SuperGal vs. GOD

second edition

BIBLE STUDY &
BOOK CLUB GUIDE

PEOPLE ARE SAYING ...

Raves for *SuperGal vs. GOD*

Awarded "Book of the Year 2014 / Biography, Memoir"
—*Christian Small Publishers' Association.*

"A woman's faith is sorely tested in this sprightly, tragicomic novel of redemption ... In Hynson's deftly comic prose, Lori is a charming protagonist ... As readers watch her do battle with God, they may not be able to help siding with the underdog. A winsome, entertaining and occasionally inspiring story of bad things happening to pretty good people.
—*Kirkus Reviews*

"God, Satan and the author fight for control in this fun and dramatic memoir ... Any woman who has struggled with the ups and downs of being an independent, overworked and underappreciated superwoman may see herself in this well-written and inspirational memoir."
—*Clarion Reviews*

PUBLISHED BY: Elk Lake Publishing, Inc., 35 Dogwood Dr., Plymouth, MA 02360, 2019

Library Cataloging Data

Names: Hynson, Lori and Hynson, Diana L. (*Lori Hynson and Diana L Hynson*)

SuperGal vs GOD Bible Study & Book Club Guide / Lori Hynson and Diana L. Hynson

66 p. 23cm × 15cm (9in × 6 in.)

Description: SuperGal, Lori, overachieves as a matter of course. Self-confidence to the hilt, she can do anything she sets her mind to. Until she finds she cannot control the health of the man she's come to love and is driven to the point where the only one who can help is God.

Identifiers: ISBN-13: 978-1-950051-80-9 (trade) | 978-1-950051-81-6 (POD)

| 978-1-950051-82-3 (e-book)

Key Words: perfectionism, overachievement, divorce, love story, God in action, self-confident, self esteem

LCCN: 2019xxxxxx Nonfiction

Super Gal vs. GOD

second edition

BIBLE STUDY & BOOK CLUB GUIDE

LORI HYNSON

DIANA L. HYNSON

PUBLISHING THE POSITIVE

ELK LAKE PUBLISHING INC.
Plymouth, Massachusetts

TABLE OF CONTENTS

INTRODUCTION

This study guide is intended as a help for small group reflection and discussion. Ideally, each participant should have her or his own copy of the book. Please take time to read this introduction to the study guide, especially if you are a new group leader. **Each of the sessions assumes a group time of 60–90 minutes;** adjust as needed for your group.

For helps to use with a one-session book group discussion, see the separate Book Group Guide or choose from among the questions and activities in these sessions.

THE SESSIONS AND APPROACHES

The Guide includes six sessions, each covering several chapters. There is plenty to chew on in each chapter, so you may decide to divide one or more of the sessions. (There are suggested break points in the session plans.) Each session includes commentary and activities that lead to discussion. These will elicit similar experiences and stories among the group members.

SELECTING ACTIVITIES

Choose which questions and/or activities you will use based on your knowledge of the group and the time allotted for the session. Remember that activities take longer to explain and do than the questions alone. You are encouraged to stretch a bit beyond your comfort zone and try activities that you may never have used before.

USING SCRIPTURE

There are numerous Scripture citations in the book as well as added references in the study material. Use whatever translation of the Bible you wish, though it would be best to use only versions that are *translations* (as opposed to *paraphrases*, such as *The Message*). For the best discussion, encourage the use of several translations to explore the different nuances that can be gained from the various scholarly approaches taken in those translations. For copyright purposes, you will find the biblical reference only, rather than the text, printed in the study guide, so each participant should have and use their own Bible.

SHARING LEADERSHIP

If you use a team approach to each session, be sure that all team leaders have a copy of this study guide and are clear about their own responsibilities for the session. Plan together which questions and activities you will use and who will lead them. Changing your approach, pace, or leader each fifteen minutes or so helps keep the group members engaged.

If leadership rotates from session to session, help the leader of the next session know where you left off, especially if you want to continue working with the same session at the next meeting time. Plan together how you will maintain the continuity and flow of the session from one meeting time to the next. You will need to add the devotional time and music for the second part of a divided session.

ADVANCE SESSION PREPARATION

Read the relevant chapters in *SuperGal vs. GOD*. Review and select the questions and activities that fit your time and group. (Remember that a SuperGal would try new things!) Choose an alternative or two, just in case something doesn't work or you have extra time. Gather the supplies and materials from the list for your selected activities and print copies of the Participant Page(s) for the session. Select the music you will use, if any.

Think about your meeting space. What can you bring or do to make it feel like a sacred, hospitable, comfortable, and safe place? (You might have a candle or other symbols to point to the presence of God, beverages or other light refreshments, name tags, and so on.)

Pray for your group members.

LEADING THE GROUP SESSION

Group members contribute more easily if they have their own copy of the discussion questions or other instructions, which are conveniently printed on the separate Participant Pages. These handouts should be copied and distributed for use in educational settings, and they will save the time it takes to repeat questions or explanations.

The sessions are not scripted, but the instructions are complete and addressed to the group leader. The discussions questions are directed to "you" (the group member).

Begin and end your session with prayer and if possible, with one or two hymns or songs relating to the suggested theme of the session.

Be open and encourage openness among group members when sharing experiences and feelings. Lori's story can elicit painful and poignant memories, so it is essential to create a safe place to think and talk about them. (Do not try to fix, counsel, or argue with anyone.) Make sure that the more reticent members of the group have an opportunity to contribute and that the more talkative members share the discussion with others.

Hold God close; be held close by God and one another; and have fun!

SUPERGAL VS GOD BIBLE STUDY GUIDE

SESSION 1

PREPARATION

Read Chapters 1–6 and select your activities. If you divide this session, stop with Activity 3.

Gather supplies: nametags; a talking stick (a small item, like a cross or figurine that can be passed from participant to participant to give them the floor); extra copies of the book to be sure everyone has a copy.

Print the Participant Pages.

Set up your meeting space and arrange for music, if any.

Pray for your group members.

Lead the Session

Greet everyone and invite introductions. Use nametags if needed.

Distribute books, if needed, or tell participants how to obtain one.

Begin with prayer for group members to open their hearts and minds to the leading of the Holy Spirit.

Sing a hymn or song that invokes the power of the Holy Spirit.

Briefly introduce Chapters 1–6 if participants have not read them in advance. Chapters 1 and 2 provide some family background information, and we meet "SuperGal." Chapters 3–6 introduce Lori's early foray into a formal church setting. Distribute the Participant Page.

Activity 1: Get acquainted. Give group members one minute to jot down some of the family-of-origin experiences that they are willing to share and that they believe have helped to form them as they are today. Then use a talking stick to have them take **no more than three minutes** each to mention those experiences. Monitor this activity so it doesn't get away from you.

Activity 2: Read Galatians 5:16–26. Paul contrasts "works of the flesh" (meaning things that debase ourselves or others) and "works of the Spirit" (meaning things that edify and lift up). We know we engage in both works, sometimes within minutes of each other. Use the talking stick to guide the flow of conversation and ask:

How do these "works of the flesh" interfere with "inheriting the kingdom of God?" What does it mean to "inherit the Kingdom?"

How does held anger, quarrels, jealousy, and the like form an identity?

How does the way we manifest the "fruit of the Spirit" (v 22) form an identity?

Activity 3: Explore your own light and shadows. Lori mentions her SuperGal gifts and strengths and also the Shadow face:

Go-getter, reliable, energetic, confident, committed versus big ego, selfish, resentful, over-achieving, giving family the leftovers, and so on. (See Chapter 2.) Consider your notes and conversation from Activities 1 and 2 and have group members identify the gifts and shadows in their own lives. Then discuss these questions:

What are the gifts and strengths that are at the heart of your identity?

How do those gifts and strengths sustain you?

How much of a SuperGal or SuperGuy are you? How do those traits help you to be your best self? How do they interfere?

If there is a shadow side to your gifts and strengths, how is it exhibited?

What do you do (or could you do) to "lighten" that shadow side?

Activity 4: Consider the wisdom of C.S.Lewis. In Chapter 3, Lori says "I thought of myself as a Christian, pretty much," but also adds "why bother God with my problems?" In essence, this is practical atheism—claiming belief, but acting otherwise. Read the quote by C.S. Lewis on the introduction page to Part One in the book and then ask:

Where do you see yourself in Lori or Lewis's descriptions? If you lean to "practical atheist," how does it fit with your understanding and exercise of your gifts and strengths?

Is dependence on God the same as weakness? Why or why not?

Activity 5: Think about how you "do church." In Chapters 4–6, Lori writes about her experience of "church shopping," the early days of attending Second Baptist, and her baptism. Take a few minutes to think first about how newcomers are welcomed and incorporated into your worshipping community and about how they are prepared for baptism and/or church membership. Focus on what is actually done, not what you wish could be done. Then discuss these questions:

What does your congregation do before the worship service starts? Who welcomes "Lori?" How would Lori be greeted and by whom?

How are newcomers put at ease?

How do congregational practices and the facility help visitors follow what is going on (or not) and get where they need to go?

What assumptions are made before and during worship about what worshippers know?

If a visitor is from a different racial or cultural group, is he or she treated differently than "one of your own?" If so, how? (This can be very subtle.)

When a newcomer decides to join, what plans and practices are in place? Have you ever evaluated them to find out if they work the way you want?

What attention is paid to education, acculturation, insider language, and other church-specific issues that may be foreign to a newcomer? What assumptions do you make about these issues? What might you do differently?

The Second Baptist choir members immediately saw the need and opportunity to become "family" for Lori at her baptism. How, especially in larger churches, do you form groups and relationships that are personal and safe?

Close the session. Thank participants for coming and ask them to read Chapters 7–15 for Session Two (unless you have divided this session.) Offer a benediction.

SESSION ONE PARTICIPANT PAGE

Activity 2: Galatians 5:16–26

How do these "works of the flesh" interfere with "inheriting the kingdom of God?" What does it mean to "inherit the Kingdom?"

How does held anger, quarrels, jealousy, and the like form an identity?

How does the way we manifest the "fruit of the Spirit" (v 22) form an identity?

Activity 3: Explore your own light and shadows

What are the gifts and strengths that are at the heart of your identity?

How do those gifts and strengths sustain you?

How much of a SuperGal or SuperGuy are you? How do those traits help you to be your best self? How do they interfere?

If there is a shadow side to your gifts and strengths, how is it exhibited?

What do you do (or could you do) to "lighten" that shadow side?

Activity 4: Consider the wisdom of C.S. Lewis

Where do you see yourself in Lori or C.S. Lewis' descriptions? If you lean to "practical atheist," how does it fit with your understanding and exercise of your gifts and strengths?

Is dependence on God the same as weakness? Why or why not?

Activity 5: Think about how do you "do church"

What does your congregation do before the worship service starts? Who welcomes "Lori?" How would Lori be greeted and by whom?

How are newcomers put at ease?

How do congregational practices and the facility help visitors follow what is going on (or not) and get where they need to go?

What assumptions are made before and during worship about what worshippers know?

If a visitor is from a different racial or cultural group, is he or she treated differently than "one of your own?" If so, how? (This can be very subtle.)

When a newcomer decides to join, what plans and practices are in place? Have you ever evaluated them to find out if they work the way you want?

What attention is paid to education, acculturation, insider language, and other church-specific issues that may be foreign to a newcomer? What assumptions do you make about these issues? What might you do differently?

The Second Baptist choir members immediately saw the need and opportunity to become "family" for Lori at her baptism. How, especially in larger churches, do you form groups and relationships that are personal and safe places to learn and grow?

SESSION TWO

PREPARATION

Read Chapters 7–15 and select your activities. If you divide this session, stop with Activity 5.

Gather your supplies: nametags, if needed; a talking stick; art supplies; Bibles

Print the Participant Pages.

Set up your meeting space and arrange for music, if any.

Pray for your group members.

Lead the Session

Welcome everyone and begin with a brief devotional. Pray with the group to be open to God's voice, nudges, and miracles.

Sing together a hymn or song of devotion.

Distribute the Participant Pages.

Prepare with Scripture.

Activity 1: Read Exodus 3:1–4:17. Moses turned aside to marvel at a burning bush (a BIG nudge and bigger voice) and God spoke to him, calling him to be God's agent in freeing the Hebrews from slavery in Egypt. Moses repeatedly put up excuses until he pushed God to anger. Talk about the flow and action of the Exodus story and then make it personal.

When have you had a conviction, but not the courage of it? How did it feel to know what was right to do, but not have the wherewithal to follow through?

What "tools" did God place before Moses? And before you, when you have had a" burning bush" experience? What did you do with them?

Activity 2: Watch for the voice, the nudge, and the miracle. In these beginning chapters and throughout the book, Lori speaks about learning to recognize the presence of God in various voices, nudges, and miracles, many times only in hindsight.

Divide into three subgroups. Skim these chapters looking for instances of the voice (group one), nudges (group two) and inklings of miracles (group three). Allow 10–15 minutes for the subgroups to skim, compare impressions among themselves, and jot down notes. **Use the prompts for each subgroup on the Participant Pages** to aid the review. Bring the whole group together for discussion, using the talking stick, if you wish.

Activity 3: Consider the meadowlark. The story of the meadowlark is a cautionary tale or parable. Read the story on pages 58–59 in the book. (Patti LuPone's rendering is wonderful and adds another dimension to the story. You can find the recording on YouTube.) If nothing else, the story reminds us that decisions have consequences, and ones that can affect others beyond ourselves.

What, do you think, are the intended and unintended consequences of the meadowlark's decision?

In this case, the gift also came with sacrifice. When have you been faced with your own "meadowlark" moments? How did you explore your options and decide what path to take?

In light of what Lori says in the several pages following that story, what, would you say, were her "meadowlark" moments?

What voice, nudge, or miracle was (or may have been) concealed in your own "meadowlark" moments or in Lori's?

Activity 4: Yep—you can do theology. Lori alludes to theological beliefs, thinking, and comments, even though she probably didn't identify them that way at the time.

"When it comes to forgiveness, God doesn't rub it in—He rubs it out!" (p 61).

"Satan spotted activity at SuperGal's house ..."

"The Holy Spirit whispered to SuperGal ..."

"SuperGal prayed because it comforted her, not because she expected resolution from someone other than herself" (p 63).

"God stood by waiting... He was patient. She didn't deserve it."

"[Conrad's] ... trust in God in the face of this tragedy confused me." (p 67).

Lori, at this functionally "pre-Christian" stage, had untested and perhaps uninformed ideas about God and so seemed not to understand or to be able to accept grace from God (as in forgiveness or patience). How do you (or your church) recognize the signs of this kind of theological simplicity and mentor those who are not so far along on their journey of Christian formation? What obligation do you have to be a mentor? (Think back to Moses when you answer!)

In what ways is Lori seeing God (in all God's persons) at work? Is this familiar to you? How do you see God working in your life?

What do these theological "revelations" also say about your relationship to God?

We think of God as a personage, but these remarks also personalize the Holy Spirit and Satan. Who (or what) are the Holy Spirit and Satan to you?

Conrad probably didn't have any idea at the time what sort of a model he was for Lori. How did he help her, if only unknowingly? What awareness do you have of how you model the faith for people whom you don't realize are even paying attention? What obligation does your faith place upon you to take responsibility for the faith formation of others?

Activity 5: Enter Ben. Lori offers here a clear portrait of ambivalence: interested, not interested; come hither, back off; intrigued, frightened; never again, what's next? Imagine yourselves as Ben and Lori's friend, invisibly watching these encounters and being able to read the little "thought bubbles" over each one's head that neither Ben nor Lori could see.(That's funnier than the limerick about Ethel Merman!)

Distribute paper and some simple drawing implements. Ask group members to think about one of these encounters (such as, at Amelie's, p. 70; at the car, pp 71–72; at the Ethel Merman poem, p 72–73; at Thanksgiving dinner and weekend, pp 99–100; or other incidents in Chapters 12–15). Label the encounter, draw it simply (stick figures are fine), fill in thought bubbles above the action and the real conversation at the bottom of the page, and then have a little fun at their expense seeing the disconnections and misdirections.

Do "show and tell" with your artwork, then discuss these questions.

How do you navigate new relationships when conversation is more protected and less candid?

How do you recognize and deal with the subtext in conversations, especially when the subtext is more truthful or revealing than the spoken words?

What do you do when you see that your own or the other's inner voice is trying to torpedo what is going on?

How does "SuperGal-ness" (or SuperGuy-ness) help and hinder your relationships with others?

Lori wasn't sure if "cupid juice" was harmful to SuperGals. What would you say to her and why?

Activity 6: A storm's brewing. On page 100, Lori says, "SuperGal was an enigma. To the world, she was assertive and strong. Independent. Behind closed doors she was hopelessly bound by the emotional chains she had forged all on her own." That's a storm recipe, regardless of what is going on, and a big battle was about to begin.

Together summarize how the stage has been set to meet the storm and how one's understanding of oneself and God provides ammunition (either for God or "Satan," as it has been staged here).

Close the session. Thank participants for coming and ask them to read Chapters 16–22 for the next session (unless you have divided this session.) Remind them to bring their Bible. Offer a benediction.

SESSION TWO PARTICIPANT PAGES

Activity 1: Prepare with Scripture—Exodus 3:1–4:17

When have you had a conviction, but not the courage of it? How did it feel to know what was right to do, but not have the wherewithal to follow through?

What "tools" did God place before Moses? And before you, when you have had a "burning bush" experience? What did you do with them?

Activity 2: Watch for the voice, the nudge, and the miracle

The Voice (Prompts for subgroup one)

In what ways is God's voice communicated? In what circumstances?

There are instances of both hearing the voice of God and of finding one's own voice. How different is that?

Where are the points of resistance, and what feeds the resistance?

Nudges (Prompts for subgroup two)

What nudges do you see and what form do they take? What are the circumstances?

Sometimes the nudge to someone else is crystal clear but our own are only murky. What, do you think, made Lori open (or not) to these nudges?

How is the cognitive dissonance handled (when your brain is going in many different directions and things should, but don't seem to make sense)?

Miracles (Prompts for subgroup three)

What, do you think, is a miracle as opposed to "magic?" (See Lori's comment on page 57 about wanting things to change by magic.)

When might some extraordinary happening be called a miracle?

In what ways does/can God convey a miracle?

Who has helped Lori recognize the extravagant activity of God?

Activity 3: Consider the meadowlark

What, do you think, are the intended and unintended consequences of the meadowlark's decision?

In this case, the gift also came with sacrifice. When have you been faced with your own "meadowlark" moments? How did you explore your options and decide what path to take?

In light of what Lori says in the several pages following that story, what, would you say, were her "meadowlark" moments?

What Voice, nudge, or miracle was (or may have been) concealed in your own meadowlark moments or Lori's?

Activity 4: Yep; you can do theology

"When it comes to forgiveness, God doesn't rub it in—He rubs it out!" (p 61)

"Satan spotted activity at SuperGal's house ..."

"The Holy Spirit whispered to SuperGal ..."

"SuperGal prayed because it comforted her, not because she expected resolution from someone other than herself." (p 63)

"God stood by waiting ... He was patient. She didn't deserve it."

"[Conrad's] ... trust in God in the face of this tragedy confused me." (p 67).

Lori, at this functionally "pre-Christian" stage, had untested and perhaps uninformed ideas about God and so seemed not to understand or to be able to accept grace from God (as in forgiveness or patience). How do you (or your church) recognize the signs of this kind of theological simplicity and mentor those who are not so far along on their journey of Christian formation? What obligation do you have to be a mentor? (Think back to Moses when you answer!)

In what ways is Lori seeing God (in all God's persons) at work? Is this familiar to you? How do you see God working in your life?

What do these theological "revelations" also say about your relationship to God?

We think of God as a personage, but these remarks also personalize the Holy Spirit and Satan. Who (or what) are the Holy Spirit and Satan to you?

Conrad probably didn't have any idea at the time what sort of a model he was for Lori. How did he help her, if only unknowingly? What awareness do you have of how you model the faith for people whom you don't realize are even paying attention?

Activity 5: Enter Ben

Think about one of Ben and Lori's first encounters (such as, at Amalie's, p 70; at the car, pp 71–72; at the Ethel Merman poem, pp 72–73; at Thanksgiving dinner and weekend, pp 99–100; or other incidents in Chapters 12–15). Label the encounter, draw it simply (stick figures are fine), fill in thought bubbles above the action and the real conversation at the bottom of the page, and then have notice the disconnections and misdirections.

How do you navigate new relationships when conversation is more protected and less candid?

How do you recognize and deal with the subtext in conversations, especially when the subtext is more truthful or revealing than the spoken words?

What do you do when you see that your own or the other's inner voice is trying to torpedo what is going on?

How does "SuperGal-ness" (or SuperGuy-ness) help and hinder your relationships with others?

Lori wasn't sure if "cupid juice" was harmful to SuperGals. What would you say to her and why?

Activity 6: A storm's brewing

Together summarize how the stage has been set to meet the storm and how one's understanding of oneself and God provides ammunition (either for God or "Satan," as it's been staged here).

SESSION THREE

PREPARATION

Read Chapters 16–22 and select your activities.
Gather supplies: Bibles, talking stick
Print the Participant Page.
Set up your meeting space and arrange for music, if any.
Pray for your group members.

Lead the Session
Welcome everyone and begin with a brief devotional. Pray with the group to be open to the gifts of being in a supportive community.
Sing together a hymn or song of devotion.
Distribute the Participant Page.

Activity 1: The battle begins. These chapters run from the insecurity of "Why hasn't he called?" to "Can this get any worse?" The first battle, it would seem, was one of the heart. In Chapters 16 and 17, Lori is forced to realize and admit her true feelings and also to confront and contain her SuperGal tendencies. Discuss together:

Have you had your own "wake up call" that helped you see something important more clearly? What form did it take? Did you consider it to be a nudge from God?

Have you had your own experience of discovering how you felt about someone or something because you were (or may have been) on the brink of losing it? If you did lose it, how did you cope with your feelings? If you didn't, how did that shape your future behavior, feelings, and attitudes?

Note the several awkward moments and imagine how you may have felt and what you thought would be prudent to do or say.

Activity 2: Where's the cavalry? Read 1 Corinthians 10:12–13. This is one snippet in a longer commentary about the danger of idolatry. One form of idolatry, perhaps the most prevalent, is thinking ourselves to be more powerful than God. A crucial point about this passage is that the "you" is plural. Paul is speaking to the entire community, not just to an individual. When one member of the community is burdened, God working through the community supports that individual.

Lori mentions on page 113 that she felt strangely removed from her own family and friends; on pages 109-110, having to call Kelly and Joe, whom she did not know; and on page 133, fearing an interrogation or interview from Diana at their first meeting. Furthermore, on page 115, Lori (or is that SuperGal?) seems to be blaming herself somehow that Ben is getting worse instead of better. Yet on meeting Ben's family, Lori found them to be treasured allies. Think about these questions:

Have you had to call upon strangers or infrequent acquaintances to be community for you? How did it feel? Did you see the hand of God in that situation?

When stuff has piled on, or you have piled it on yourself, do you "call out the cavalry?" Who is "cavalry" for you?

Some have said that they wished God would not think them so strong, because they didn't know how much more of a burden they could bear. How does this Scripture passage speak to you in this context?

Lori's "super" instincts had her thinking she could control and fix everything; and since they weren't fixed, it was somehow her fault. How does holding your concerns in a community help you with your perspective in those concerns?

When have you feared an "interrogation, or at least an interview" that didn't materialize? How did you feel before and after, particularly when realizing you had spent energy that way?

Activity 3: The battle heats up. In Chapters 18–20, Ben's physical crisis and Lori's emotional and spiritual crises are mounting precipitously (with much more to come). Divide the group into triads. Ask each smaller group to skim Chapters 18–20 and to make two lists in columns. In the first column, list all the theological allusions and comments and in the second column, SuperGal's actions or thoughts that either elicited the allusion or were a response to it. Give groups several minutes to work on their lists.

Then have the small groups designate one person as "Lori" and the others as the faithful "cavalry." How might the cavalry share Scripture, words of faith and encouragement, and insight WITHOUT trying to fix or advise

Lori? In other words, the friends can't also take a stance like SuperGal. How could they help Lori see something different for herself? (This is harder than you might think, and the friends should monitor each other.)

Activity 4: Is there any benefit to prayer? Lori has mentioned numerous times the tentative ways in which she prayed and her doubt then about the efficacy of prayer, contrasted with the prayers of others; for example Diana (p 138) and Carmen and her covenant partner (p 140). Read James 1:5–8 and 4:1–3, 7–8; two passages that touch on what puts power in prayer. Think about Lori's practice then, as well as your own, in light of this Scripture. Then discuss:

What is your experience with "gimme" prayers and how well they work?

What could be considered the "right" way to pray? How do you know? What is your experience with that?

How does "worthiness" or a sense of entitlement figure into the experience of realized prayer?

Prayer is often enigmatic; we don't always know when or why God says yes to some and no to others. Given this, what makes you continue to pray or have hope in prayer?

Close the session. Thank participants for coming and ask them to read Chapters 23–30 for the next time. Remind them to bring their Bible. Offer a benediction.

SESSION THREE PARTICIPANT PAGE

Activity 1: The battle begins

Have you had your own "wake up call" that helped you see something important more clearly? What form did it take? Did you consider it to be a nudge from God?

Have you had your own experience of discovering how you felt about someone or something because you were (or may have been) on the brink of losing it? If you did lose it, how did you cope with your feelings? If you didn't, how did that shape your future behavior, feelings, and attitudes?

Note the several awkward moments and imagine how you may have felt and what you thought would be prudent to do or say.

Activity 2: Where's the cavalry?—1 Corinthians 10:12–13

Note comments on pages 113, 115, 109-110, and 133 as directed by the group leader.

Have you had to call upon strangers or infrequent acquaintances to be community for you? How did it feel? Did you see the hand of God in that situation?

When stuff has piled on, or you have piled it on yourself, do you "call out the cavalry?" Who is "cavalry" for you?

Some have said that they wished God would not think them so strong, because they didn't know how much more of a burden they could bear. How does this Scripture passage speak to you in this context?

Lori's "super" instincts had her thinking she could control and fix everything; and since they weren't fixed, it was somehow her fault. How does holding your concerns in a community help you with your perspective in those concerns?

When have you feared an "interrogation, or at least an interview" that didn't materialize? How did you feel before and after, particularly when realizing you had spent energy that way?

Activity 3: The battle heats up

Within your small group, list in one column all the theological allusions and comments and in a second column, SuperGal's actions or thoughts that either elicited the allusion or were a response to it. Afterward, one person is "Lori" and the others are the faithful "cavalry." The cavalry will share Scripture, words of faith and encouragement, and insight WITHOUT trying to fix or advise Lori to help Lori see something different for herself. (This is harder than you might think, and the friends should monitor each other.)

Activity 4: Is there any benefit to prayer?—James 1:5–8 and 4:1–3, 7–8

Note also comments on pages 138 and 140.

What is your experience with "gimme" prayers and how well they work?

What could be considered the "right" way to pray? How do you know? What is your experience with that?

How does "worthiness" or a sense of entitlement figure into the experience of realized prayer? How about bargaining?

Prayer is often enigmatic; we don't always know when or why God says yes to some and no to others. Given this, what makes you continue to pray or have hope in prayer?

SESSION FOUR

PREPARATION

Read Chapters 23–30 and select your activities. If you divide this session, stop with Activity 2.

Gather supplies: Bibles, talking stick, a hymnal or book of worship that contains your baptismal liturgy; Walter Salman's picture of Jesus at the door; an iPad or other device to show the picture. (Search on the internet for the art.)

Print the Participant Pages.

Set up your meeting space and arrange for music, if any.

Pray for your group members.

Lead the Session

Welcome everyone and begin with a brief devotional. Pray with the group to be open to God's direction and messengers.

Sing together a hymn or song of trust and obedience.

Distribute the Participant Pages.

Activity 1: January 6: One terrible day. Chapters 23–24 take us through January 6. Notice the mounting frustration, fear, and anger in these chapters (Lori wasn't the only one!) as well as the nudges. Then consider these questions:

Focusing on negativity (also called "downward spiral thinking") is understandable in the midst of such turmoil, but it is not helpful. What specific instances do you see of this downward spiral? What, if anything, helped to mitigate it?

Think about your own approach to life's turmoil and difficulties. How much provocation does it take for you to slip into downward spiral thinking? If you get in that mode, what does it take to get you out?

Lori didn't recognize the first messenger, but other messages were chipping away at SuperGal's wall of stubbornness. What were they?

January 6, Epiphany, celebrates the revelation of God through Jesus Christ, specifically in the visit of the Magi (Matthew 2) and in Jesus' baptism. Review Matthew 3:13–17 and the baptismal liturgy in your hymnal or book of worship. Lori wondered if her own baptism mattered (p 168). What do the baptismal vows that you made, or were made on your behalf, mean to you? Do they sustain you in any way? If so, how?

Activity 2: One does what one can. In Chapters 25–27, Lori devised her Plans A (ambush the doctor!) and B (enlist the nurses). Kelly had a plan also (*No Children, No Pets,* weekly visits, and the assumption of financial duties), and then there was Little Man. Lori and Kelly both worked on "technical fixes": specific "mechanical" tasks needed to be tended, and they were. But sometimes an issue is "adaptive"; that is, it requires non-rational, non-linear, non-mechanical flexibility, and the goal is not to fix, but to respond with creativity. Furthermore, we cannot effectively apply a technical fix to an adaptive issue and expect good results, because it doesn't work.

What were the technical fixes and the adaptive tactics in these chapters (and prior ones, if you recall)? What, do you suppose, were the outcomes (or goals)?

When have you beaten your head against a wall by continuing to force a technical fix onto an adaptive issue? Has it ever really worked satisfactorily?

In the face of these seemingly helpless, out-of-control circumstances, friends standing in the wings are eager to do something (anything!) to be useful and feel included. You have probably been such a friend. If you sincerely offered help that was never accepted, how did that make you feel?

If you have been on Lori's side, how did you regard these offers of help? If you persisted in trying to control and do everything, did you have any idea that you might actually have been hurtful to yourself or others?

Sometimes being ill, incapacitated, or very vulnerable teaches us valuable lessons about the gifts of giving and receiving. When Kelly was in hospice care in early 2013, Ben brought in *No Children, No Pets* and read it to her. Have you ever had this kind of "turnabout" experience? If so, what insights came to you? What did you learn? What attitudes or behaviors have you altered as a result?

Activity 3: February 2: Another terrible day. Chapter 28 covers February 2 when Lori was feeling really desperate, and Ben's condition was even more desperate. Quickly identify comments in the chapter that reveal this growing despair.

Form smaller groups of three or four—each to consider Psalm 23. Lift up different comments from this chapter of the book (in any order), and respond to them with each verse of the psalm. (For example, pair the telling phrase from page 174, "SuperGal was pumped and ready to rumble" with the response, "The LORD is my shepherd.") Allow time for subgroups to work, then come together and compare your psalmody.

Activity 4: A dark night. Review Chapter 29. Examine the Scriptures, the messenger's witness, and SuperGal's perception of the failure of God, prayer, and her own best efforts (pp 181-182). Consider these questions:

What were SuperGal's best efforts and how could they contribute to Ben's recovery? If we are a "resurrection people" would Ben's death be a failure?

Have you ever tried, time and again, to offer words of encouragement or guidance to someone only to have it consistently resisted and refused? What was that like? What made you decide either to continue or give up?

In what ways do we create situations (consciously or unconsciously) in which what we fear is what comes to pass?

Have you "entertained an angel, unaware?" What opened your awareness?

Activity 5: Then the dawn. Have the picture of Jesus at the door for display and review Chapter 30. Read the Scriptures mentioned there, as well as Revelation 3:14–22. Focus first on the third messenger (pp 188-191). One thing that was different about his message is that in addition to telling SuperGal what God can do, he revealed the one thing SuperGal's best efforts had not yet done: to be grateful, and why. Consider these questions:

SuperGal sincerely felt she was giving her all, but had actually been "lukewarm" in some ways (see Rev. 3). How did an "attitude of gratitude" make a difference?

As you look at the picture of Jesus, you notice that the door handle cannot be seen. How might that characterize the ministry of Christ? How might that be symbolic (or telling) for your own faith journey?

The maintenance man was sent to fix a door that wouldn't open, and he did—both for the hospital and for Lori. Have you ever received that sort of messenger who helped things suddenly become open and clear for you? What was that experience like? Was there any alteration to your attitudes, beliefs, or behavior? If so, did it last?

The maintenance man also pointed out *why* she should be grateful; not just something else to do. It was an adaptive approach, not the typical technical one. What difference does this make in any appeal? When you supply the *why* in other situations, to what are you appealing? How often and well does it work?

Activity 6: Goodbye, SuperGal? Review pages 192-196 and discuss these questions:

Have you ever prayed a prayer of relinquishment—"Thy will be done"—and then really let go? How did it feel? What did it accomplish? If you took back that burden over time, what happened?

Do ever get in your own way? If so, how do you figure out how to step aside?

Close the session. Thank participants for coming and ask them to read Chapters 31–39 (all of Part Three) for the next time, unless you have divided this session. Remind them to bring their Bible. Offer a benediction.

SESSION FOUR PARTICIPANT PAGES

Activity 1: January 6—One terrible day

Focusing on negativity (also called "downward spiral thinking") is understandable in the midst of such turmoil, but it is not helpful. What specific instances to you see of this downward spiral? What, if anything, helped to mitigate it?

Think about your own approach to life's turmoil and difficulties. How much provocation does it take for you to slip into downward spiral thinking? If you get in that mode, what does it take to get you out?

Lori didn't recognize the first messenger, but other messages were chipping away at SuperGal's wall of stubbornness. What were they?

January 6, Epiphany, celebrates the revelation of God through Jesus Christ. One related Scripture is the story of Jesus' baptism. Review Matthew 3:13–17 and the baptismal liturgy in your hymnal or book of worship. Lori wondered if her own baptism mattered (p 168). What do the baptismal vows that you made, or were made on your behalf, mean to you? Do they sustain you in any way? If so, how?

Activity 2: One does what one can

What were the technical fixes and the adaptive tactics in these chapters (and prior ones, if you recall)? What, do you suppose, were the outcomes (or goals)?

When have you beaten your head against a wall by continuing to force a technical fix onto an adaptive issue? Has it ever really worked satisfactorily?

In the face of these seemingly helpless, out of control circumstances, friends standing in the wings are eager to do something (anything!) to be useful and feel included. You have probably been such a friend. If you sincerely offered help that was never accepted, how did that make you feel?

If you have been on Lori's side, how did you regard these offers of help? If you persisted in trying to control and do everything, did you have any idea that you might actually have been hurtful to yourself or others?

Sometimes being ill, incapacitated, or very vulnerable teaches us valuable lessons about the gifts of giving and receiving. When Kelly was in hospice care in early 2013, Ben brought in *No Children, No Pets* and read it to her. Have you ever had this kind of "turnabout" experience? If so, what insights came to you? What did you learn? What attitudes or behaviors have you altered as a result?

Activity 3: February 2—Another terrible day

In your small group consider Psalm 23. Lift up different comments from this chapter of the book (in any order), and respond to them with each verse of the psalm. (For example, pair the telling phrase from page 174, "SuperGal was pumped and ready to rumble" with the response, "The LORD is my shepherd.")

Activity 4: A dark night

What were SuperGal's best efforts and how could they contribute to Ben's recovery? If we are a "resurrection people" would Ben's death be a failure?

Have you ever tried, time and again, to offer words of encouragement or guidance to someone only to have it consistently resisted and refused? What was that like? What made you decide to either continue or give up?

In what ways do we create situations (consciously or unconsciously) in which what we fear is what comes to pass?

Have you "entertained an angel, unaware?" What opened your awareness?

Activity 5: Then the dawn

SuperGal sincerely felt she was giving her all, but had actually been "lukewarm" in some ways (see Rev. 3). How did an "attitude of gratitude" make a difference?

As you look at the picture of Jesus, you notice that the door handle cannot be seen. How might that characterize the ministry of Christ? How might that be symbolic (or telling) for your own faith journey?

The maintenance man was sent to fix a door that wouldn't open, and he did—both for the hospital and for Lori. Have you ever received that sort of messenger who helped things suddenly become open and clear for you?

What was that experience like? Was there any alteration to your attitudes, beliefs, or behavior? If so, did it last?

The maintenance man also pointed out *why* she should be grateful; not just something else to do. It was an adaptive approach, not the typical technical one. What difference does this make in any appeal? When you supply the *why* in other situations, to what are you appealing? How often and well does it work?

Activity 6: Goodbye, SuperGal?

Have you ever prayed a prayer of relinquishment—"Thy will be done"—and then really let go? How did it feel? What did it accomplish? If you took back that burden over time, what happened?

Do ever get in your own way? If so, how do you figure out how to step aside?

SESSION FIVE

Preparation

Read Chapters 31–39 and select your activities. If you divide this session, stop with Activity 3.

Gather supplies: Bibles, talking stick

Print the Participant Pages.

Set up your meeting space and arrange for music, if any.

Pray for your group members.

Lead the Session

Welcome everyone and begin with a brief devotional. Pray with the group, giving thanks for God's power and grace.

Sing together a hymn or song of confidence in time of trial.

Distribute the Participant Pages.

Activity 1: Lori up; Ben down. The last session ended with Lori's epiphany of God's presence and grace, while Ben's physical condition, after a brief improvement, grew more precarious, then came to a critical head. But SuperGal's false sense of power is being replaced with the acceptance of God's strength. Briefly review the events in these chapters, without discussing them, and then look at the numerous sustaining quotes, Scriptures, and anecdotes. (Divide them among group members, if you wish.) Before delving into these quotes, read aloud John 14: 25–26, which affirms that it is the Holy Spirit who brings to remembrance the Word and words God wants us to recall.

Song, pp 203-204
Miller, p 205
Hugo, p 205
Tennyson, p 206

How is God at work through these words and events?

What do these quotes and experiences evoke in you? How do they influence your own story?

When you have been faced with trying times, do you find that words, stories, and/or other memories poke their way into your consciousness? If so, what has happened and how did it influence you?

Music is very evocative. If hymns or other music comes to mind, sing a little bit of it together and talk about how it is sustaining or comforting.

When you come upon "words to live by" do you have a method of planting them firmly in your memory? What do you do?

Activity 2: More internal struggle. At the end of Chapter 30, Lori had given SuperGal the boot. On page 211, we see SuperGal trying to win her way back in. By pages 219-220, Lori is beginning to sort herself out. Skim over those pages and then discuss:

What happens to you if you try to deny the "unlovely" parts of yourself?

How or when can your weaknesses also be your strengths? Conversely, when are your strengths also your weaknesses?

What do you do to work on keeping yourself wholly integrated; that is, using all of your traits, behaviors, and habits in healthy ways?

Some of this struggle is presented as being in contention with "Satan"—the internal trash-talking, second-guessing, and self-doubt. On page 227, Lori asks herself, "whose voice would [she] heed?" What do you do when this nasty internal battle occurs within yourself? How often do you succumb to "Satan's" voice? What pulls you back to a better place?

Who helps you to see when you are disintegrated? Do you listen to them?

Activity 3: April 9–11: Yet other terrible days. Review Chapters 36–37, which relate the build-up to the worst crisis yet. Have group members read all of Esther 4. It is no wonder that Lori likens the situation with Ben to this: a life-or-death decision must be made. Ask:

What are the factors here that cause anguish?

What are the positive and courageous undercurrents?

If you have been in "just such a time as this," how did you handle it? What voices did you heed? Which did you ignore? What helped you decide?

On page 250, Lori begins to review the pile of miracles and nudges that brought them to this decision point, only this time, she sees herself not as the instigator, but as God's helper. Have you ever had a powerful feeling that you were God's agent in something big or special? What happened?

Activity 4: April 12: The big day. Chapters 38–39 relate the day of surgery, which found and fixed the festering, hidden problem that would never otherwise have allowed Ben to heal. That day, and the days before, and the days after were filled with prayers, spoken and unspoken. Pages 254 and 255 relates instances of praying *for* and praying *with*. Consider these questions:

Ben was disappointed that the chaplain prayed silently and said "he didn't help much." Lori explained that hundreds of people (from far and wide) were covering Ben and the medical staff with prayer, yet she felt guilty and cowardly for not praying aloud with him the night before. What might this imply about the purpose and practice of prayer? About the efficacy of prayer?

Have you been asked to pray aloud for someone or some occasion? Do you feel comfortable doing that? If not, why?

Do you believe that God edits and grades your spoken prayers?

Have group members turn to the person next to them. Invite them to each make a prayer request of their partner; then take turns praying a brief prayer aloud for each other. (Practice eases discomfort!)

Activity 5: Meanwhile, back at the ranch. An unspoken part of this story is what was going on in the rest of the immediate family. Diana was waiting and praying in Tennessee, while Kelly and their mother, Helen, were doing the same in Maryland. Diana was expecting Kelly to call with the outcome of Ben's surgery and was surprised to hear from her so early in the day. As it turned out, that news was about the death of Helen's dearest friend of over sixty years. Diana left work to head to Maryland to break the news to her, grieving as well for a woman who had been an honorary aunt to her all her life and trying to anticipate how much worse her mother could feel with this heartbreak piled on top of everything else.

Beginning on pages 254–255, Lori creates a scenario of "Satan" getting his tools together to break into the hospital to wreak havoc, but found he couldn't get through God's protective barrier. Share this backstory and consider these questions:

Have you ever kept an important vigil? What did you do? How did you feel? Whose aid and comfort, if any, did you enlist?

Have you ever had multiple secondary complications in the midst of a central crisis? How did you cope with the pile of worries and concerns?

One might look at Lori's story as an experience of spiritual warfare and consider that if "Satan" couldn't get into the hospital, he chose another vulnerable place (Helen) to strike. What do you think about that?

Activity 6: Enter Helen. Another unspoken chapter is how Ben's siblings related what was going on with him to their nearly ninety-year-old mother. Helen was still in her own home, but was growing increasingly more frail; both physically and mentally. (She lived to be ninety-six!) She wanted to visit Ben, but the family demurred, considering the logistics of getting her there, how she would cope with actually seeing him so ill and hooked up to all the medical paraphernalia, and how he (and they) would cope with having to watch her cope. But, since Diana had gone home to break the news about her friend's death, she did take Helen to see Ben a few days after surgery. He looked like something from a sci-fi movie and was in a lot of pain. It wasn't pretty. Share this backstory and ask:

Have you had to figure out how to include, protect, or cope with other vulnerable family members in a difficult time? If so, how much was for their sake, and how much was for yours?

How do you decide what to say and what, if anything, to withhold?

Adults are expected to make decisions for young children and often do so for frail older adults. How do you go about respecting what those children or vulnerable adults say they want, versus what you may feel is in their best interest?

Facing difficulty is something we learn by doing, and no one can do our coping for us. How have you mentored, or been mentored by, another person in this kind of experience?

Close the session. Thank participants for coming and ask them to read Part 4 and the Epilogue for the next time, unless you have divided this session. Remind them to bring their Bible. Offer a benediction.

SESSION FIVE PARTICIPANT PAGES

Activity 1: Lori up; Ben down
Review these items.

Song, pp 203-204
Miller, p 205
Hugo, p 205
Tennyson, p 206
Unknown, p 219
ten Boom, p 225
Esther, p 234
Hebrews, p 236
Overton, p 239
Ben-Gurion, p 240
Psalm, pp 246-247
Matthew, p 247

How is God at work through these words and events? What do these quotes and experiences evoke in you? How do they influence your own story?

When you have been faced with trying times, do you find that words, stories, and/or other memories poke their way into your consciousness? If so, what has happened and how did it influence you?

Music is very evocative. If hymns or other music comes to mind, sing a little bit of it together and talk about how it is sustaining or comforting.

When you come upon "words to live by" do you have a method of planting them firmly in your memory? What do you do?

Activity 2: More internal struggle

What happens to you if you try to deny the "unlovely" parts of yourself?

How or when can your weaknesses also be your strengths? Conversely, when are your strengths also your weaknesses?

What do you do to work on keeping yourself wholly integrated; that is, using all of your traits, behaviors, and habits in healthy ways?

Some of this struggle is presented as being in contention with "Satan"—the internal trash-talking, second-guessing, and self-doubt. On page 227, Lori asks herself, "whose voice would [she] heed?" What do you do when this nasty internal battle occurs within yourself? How often do you succumb to "Satan's" voice? What pulls you back to a better place?

Who helps you to see when you are dis-integrated? Do you listen to them?

Activity 3: April 9–11—Yet other terrible days

What are the factors here that cause anguish?

What are the positive and courageous undercurrents?

If you have been in "just such a time as this," how did you handle it? What voices did you heed? Which did you ignore? What helped you decide?

On page 250, Lori begins to review the pile of miracles and nudges that brought them to this decision point, only this time, she sees herself not as the instigator, but as God's helper. Have you ever had a powerful feeling that you were God's agent in something big or special? What happened?

Activity 4: April 12—The big day

Ben was disappointed that the chaplain prayed silently and said "he didn't help much." Lori explained that hundreds of people (from far and wide) were covering Ben and the medical staff with prayer, yet she felt guilty and cowardly for not praying aloud with him the night before. What might this imply about the purpose and practice of prayer? About the efficacy of prayer?

Have you been asked to pray aloud for someone or some occasion? Do you feel comfortable doing that? If not, why?

Do you believe that God edits and grades your spoken prayers?

Turn to a person next to you. Each of you will make a prayer request of your partner; then take turns praying a brief prayer aloud for each other. (Practice eases discomfort!)

Activity 5: Meanwhile, back at the ranch

Have you ever kept an important vigil? What did you do? How did you feel? Whose aid and comfort, if any, did you enlist?

Have you ever had secondary complications in the midst of a central crisis? How did you cope with the pile of worries and concerns?

One might look at Lori's story as an experience of spiritual warfare and consider that if "Satan" couldn't get into the hospital, he chose another vulnerable place (Helen) to strike. What do you think about that?

Activity 6: Enter Helen

Have you had to figure out how to include, protect, or cope with other vulnerable family members in a difficult time? If so, how much was for their sake, and how much was for yours?

How do you decide what to say and what, if anything, to withhold?

Adults are expected to make decisions for young children and often do so for frail older adults. How do you go about respecting what those children or vulnerable adults say they want, versus what you may feel is in their best interest?

Facing difficulty is something we learn by doing, and no one can do our coping for us. How have you mentored, or been mentored by, another person in this kind of experience?

SESSION SIX

PREPARATION

Read Part 4 and the Epilogue and select your activities.
Gather supplies: Bibles, talking stick, hymnals or songbooks.
Print the Participant Page.
Set up your meeting space and arrange for music.
Pray for your group members.

Lead the Session
Welcome everyone and begin with a brief devotional. Pray with the group, giving thanks for God's healing and mercy.
Sing together a hymn or song of thanksgiving.
Distribute the Participant Page.
Activity 1: Healing begins. Chapters 40–41 relate the tentative steps toward Ben's wellness. There are a number of things happening for the first time or the first time in a long time, such as Ben's alertness and depression. Together identify others; then read together Ecclesiastes 3:1–8. Ask:

How do you find in these events (or any earlier events) the appropriate time or "season?"

Sometimes we see transitional times coming, and sometimes we don't. What helps you to recognize that a "season" is coming to a close or a new time is opening up?

So much of what we could see as the hand of God throughout these events (because she revealed it as such in the telling) was obscure to Lori until her epiphany. What part does readiness play in the advance of these times and seasons? How do you remain patient and wise when someone you know needs to hear or see, but is not ready?

On page 280, SuperGal is lecturing Lori on gratitude and obedience, rather than the other way around. (Kind of like the reformed smoker!)

Do you give yourself some credit when your weaknesses are retrained to become strengths? Without being prideful, how do you celebrate these victories?

Activity 2: Oz moments. Lori describes feeling like Dorothy on her departure from Oz when Ben was released from the hospital to rehab (p 287), but there are others through Chapters 42–43. Together, skim through them to identify other such moments. Individually or in pairs, try writing a haiku to reflect one of these moments. The pattern is three lines of five /seven / five syllables or sounds. For example: *Cast off gown and gloves / Release all your fears today / Your life lies ahead.* Allow some time to create; then compare your poetry. (If you prefer, you could try a limerick; Ben's samples are on pages 72, 73, and 83.)

After "Oz," more reality set in. Talk about these issues or questions:

Note two comments on page 289: "Anxiety has a way of prevailing over common sense ..." and "My own therapy during this time was to accept ...that I would have to loosen my grip ..." How do you give yourself space and grace to adjust in such circumstances? Do you need "permission" or help to be gentle to yourself during transition or adjustment times? Who helps you?

When Ben got home, his first question was, "Honey, who rearranged the furniture?" (p 293). What would you say to him and Lori? What "furniture" in your life needs to be rearranged? How might that process start?

Activity 3: Love, loss, joy. The Epilogue relates several instances of love, loss, and joy after Ben's homecoming, but there are numerous experiences throughout the book. As you think back over the whole story, what are the examples of love, loss, and joy that stand out as memorable, even spiritually formative, for you? Invite group members to take one or two minutes to describe these examples and think about what is the basic "takeaway" message for them.

Close with a songfest. A story with a great ending like this one needs to be celebrated, not only for the personal victories, but especially for God's victories. Distribute the hymnals or songbooks and invite group members to choose selections (or stanzas within the hymn or song) and sing them together.

Thank everyone for attending and making themselves open and vulnerable to God's activity and plan. Offer a benediction.

SESSION SIX PARTICIPANT PAGE

Activity 1: Healing begins—Ecclesiastes 3:1–8

How do you find in these events (or any earlier events) the appropriate time or "season?"

Sometimes we see transitional times coming, and sometimes we don't. What helps you to recognize that a "season" is coming to a close or a new time is opening up?

So much of what we could see as the hand of God throughout these events (because she revealed it as such in the telling) was obscure to Lori until her epiphany. What part does readiness play in the advance of these times and seasons? How do you remain patient and wise when someone you know needs to hear or see, but is not ready?

On page 280, SuperGal is lecturing Lori on gratitude and obedience, rather than the other way around. (Kind of like the reformed smoker!) Do you give yourself some credit when your weaknesses are retrained to become strengths? Without being prideful, how do you celebrate these victories?

Activity 2: Oz moments

Write a haiku to reflect one of the Oz moments. The pattern is three lines of five /seven / five syllables or sounds. For example: *Cast off gown and gloves / Release all your fears today / Your life lies ahead.* (If you prefer, you could try a limerick; Ben's samples are on pages 72, 73, and 83.)

Note two comments on page 289: "Anxiety has a way of prevailing over common sense ..." and "My own therapy during this time was to accept ... that I would have to loosen my grip ..." How do you give yourself space and grace to adjust in such circumstances? Do you need "permission" or help to be gentle to yourself during transition or adjustment times? Who helps you?

When Ben got home, his first question was, "Honey, who rearranged the furniture?" (p 293). What would you say to him and Lori? What "furniture" in your life needs to be rearranged? How might that process start?

Activity 6: Love, loss, joy

As you think back over the whole story, what are the examples of love, loss, and joy that stand out as memorable, even spiritually formative, for you? Take one or two minutes to describe these examples and think about what is the basic "takeaway" message for you.

SuperGal vs. GOD

second edition

BOOK CLUB GUIDE

PURPOSE OF THIS GUIDE

This Guide is intended for use in a one-session book club setting. The questions are taken from the longer study group format (pages 1–48). Choose from among these questions for your group or select alternates from the Study Group Guide.

Chapters 1–6

Lori mentions her SuperGal gifts and strengths and also the Shadow face: go-getter, reliable, energetic, confident, committed versus big ego, selfish, resentful, overachieving, giving family the leftovers, and so on.

How much of a SuperGal or SuperGuy are you? How do those traits help you to be your best self? How do they interfere?

If there is a shadow side to your gifts and strengths, how is it exhibited? What do you do (or could you do) to "lighten" that shadow side?

The quote by C.S. Lewis at the beginning of Part 1 says, "There are only two kinds of people in the end: those who say to God, 'Thy will be done,' and those to whom God says, in the end, '*Thy* will be done.'" Lori says, "I thought of myself as a Christian, pretty much," but also adds, "why bother God with my problems?" Lori's approach is, in essence, practical atheism.

Where do you see yourself in Lori or Lewis' descriptions? If you lean to "practical atheist," how does it fit with your understanding and exercise of your gifts and strengths? Is dependence on God the same as weakness? Why or why not?

Lori describes her experience of "church shopping."

What attention is paid at your church to education, acculturation, insider language, and other church-specific issues that may be foreign to a newcomer? What assumptions do you make about these issues? What might you do differently?

The Second Baptist choir members immediately saw the need and opportunity to become "family" for Lori at her baptism. How, especially in larger churches, do you form groups and relationships that are personal and safe?

CHAPTERS 7–13

In these chapters, and throughout the book, Lori speaks about learning to recognize the presence of God in various voices, nudges, and miracles, many times only in hindsight.

In what ways is the voice communicated? In what circumstances?

What nudges do you see and what form do they take?

What, do you think, is a miracle, as opposed to "magic?"

What, do you think, made Lori open (or not) to these voices, nudges, and miracles at this point?

Lori alludes to theological beliefs, thinking, and comments, even though she probably didn't identify them that way at the time, such as "God stood by waiting ...He was patient. She didn't deserve it" or "[Conrad's] ... trust in God in the face of this tragedy confused me."

Lori, at this functionally "pre-Christian" stage, had untested and perhaps uninformed ideas about God and so seemed not to understand or to be able to accept grace from God (as in forgiveness or patience). How do you (or your church) recognize the signs of this kind of theological simplicity and mentor those who are not so far along on their journey of Christian formation? What obligation do you have to be a mentor?

We think of God as a personage, but these remarks also personalize the Holy Spirit and Satan. Who (or what) are the Holy Spirit and Satan to you?

On page 100, Lori says, "SuperGal was an enigma. To the world, she was assertive and strong. Independent. Behind closed doors she was hopelessly bound by the emotional chains she had forged all on her own."

How has the stage been set to meet the storm that was coming, and how does one's understanding of oneself and God provides ammunition, either for God or "Satan," as it has been staged here?

CHAPTERS 16–22

These chapters run from the insecurity of "Why hasn't he called?" to "Can this get any worse?" The first battle, it would seem, was one of the heart. Lori is forced to realize and admit her true feelings and also to confront and contain her SuperGal tendencies.

Have you had your own experience of discovering how you felt about someone or something because you were (or may have been) on the brink of losing it? If you did lose it, how did you cope with your feelings? If you didn't, how did that shape your future behavior, feelings, and attitudes?

Lori mentions on page 113 that she felt strangely removed from her own family and friends; on pages 109-110, having to call Kelly and Joe, whom she did not know; and on page 133, fearing an interrogation or interview from Diana at their first meeting. Furthermore, on page 115, Lori (or is that SuperGal?) seems to be blaming herself somehow that Ben is getting worse instead of better. Yet on meeting Ben's family, Lori found them to be treasured allies.

When stuff has piled on, or you have piled it on yourself, do you "call out the cavalry?" Who is "cavalry" for you?

Lori's "super" instincts had her thinking she could control and fix everything; and since they weren't fixed, it was somehow her fault. How does holding your concerns in a community help you with your perspective in those concerns?

Lori has mentioned numerous times the tentative ways in which she prayed and her doubt then about the efficacy of prayer, contrasted with the prayers of others; for example Diana (p 138) and Carmen and her covenant partner (p 140).

What is your experience with "gimme" prayers and how well they work?

How does "worthiness" or a sense of entitlement figure into the experience of realized prayer?

Prayer is often enigmatic; we don't always know when or why God says yes to some and no to others. Given this, what makes you continue to pray or have hope in prayer?

Chapters 23–30

January 6 was an early foretaste of many terrible days to come.

Focusing on negativity (also called "downward spiral thinking") is understandable in the midst of such turmoil, but it is not helpful. What specific instances do you see of this downward spiral? What, if anything, helped to mitigate it?

Think about your own approach to life's turmoil and difficulties. How much provocation does it take for you to slip into downward spiral thinking? If you get in that mode, what does it take to get you out?

Lori and others devised their plans, which were mostly "technical"; that is, the goal was to fix something. But sometimes an issue is "adaptive"; that is, it requires non-rational, non-linear, non-technical creativity. Technical fixes for adaptive issues don't work.

When have you beaten your head against a wall by continuing to force a technical fix onto an adaptive issue? Has it ever really worked satisfactorily?

In the face of these seemingly helpless, out-of-control circumstances, friends standing in the wings are eager to do something (anything!) to be useful and feel included. You have probably been such a friend. If you sincerely offered help that was never accepted, how did that make you feel?

If you have been on Lori's side, how did you regard these offers of help? If you persisted in trying to control and do everything, did you have any idea that you might actually have been hurtful to yourself or others?

The third messenger, the maintenance man, was sent to fix a door that wouldn't open, and he did—both for the hospital and for Lori. He also pointed out *why* she should be grateful; not just something else to do. It was an adaptive approach, not the typical technical one.

Have you ever received that sort of messenger who helped things suddenly become open and clear for you? What was that experience like? Was there any alteration to your attitudes, beliefs, or behavior? If so, did it last?

What difference does the *why* make in any appeal? When you supply the *why* in other situations, to what are you appealing? How often and well does it work?

Have you ever prayed a prayer of relinquishment—"Thy will be done"—and then really let go? How did it feel? What did it accomplish? If you took back that burden over time, what happened?

Do ever get in your own way? If so, how do you figure out how to step aside?

CHAPTERS 31–39

After Lori's epiphany, Ben had a brief period of improvement, then things became critically worse, leading the surgery that finally found and fixed the internal problem. Lori mentions numerous sustaining quotes, Scriptures, and anecdotes.

When you have been faced with trying times, do you find that words, stories, songs, and/or other memories poke their way into your consciousness? If so, what has happened and how did it influence you?

When you come upon "words to live by" do you have a method of planting them firmly in your memory? What do you do?

When Lori gave this situation over to God, SuperGal got the boot temporarily, but Lori began to sort herself out.

What happens to you if you try to deny the "unlovely" parts of yourself?

What do you do to work on keeping yourself wholly integrated; that is, using all of your traits, behaviors, and habits in healthy ways?

Some of this struggle is presented as being in contention with "Satan"— the internal trash-talking, second-guessing, and self-doubt. What do you do when this nasty internal battle occurs within yourself? How often do you succumb to "Satan's" voice? What pulls you back to a better place?

On page 250, Lori begins to review the pile of miracles and nudges that brought them to this decision point, only this time, she sees herself not as the instigator, but as God's helper. Have you ever had a powerful feeling that you were God's agent in something big or special? What happened?

CHAPTERS 40–43 AND EPILOGUE

Finally, the real healing process begins.

So much of what we could see as the hand of God throughout these events (because she revealed it as such in the telling) was obscure to Lori until her epiphany. What part does readiness play in the advance of these times and seasons? How do you remain patient and wise when someone you know needs to hear or see, but is not ready?

On page 280, SuperGal is lecturing Lori on gratitude and obedience, rather than the other way around (!) Do you give yourself some credit when your weaknesses are retrained to become strengths? Without being prideful, how do you celebrate these victories?

Note two comments on page 289: "Anxiety has a way of prevailing over common sense…." and "My own therapy during this time was to accept… that I would have to loosen my grip…." How do you give yourself space and grace to adjust in such circumstances? Do you need "permission" or help to be gentle to yourself during transition or adjustment times? Who helps you?

The Epilogue relates several instances of love, loss, and joy after Ben's homecoming, but there are numerous experiences throughout the book.

As you think back over the whole story, what are the examples of love, loss, and joy that stand out as memorable, even spiritually formative, for you?

What is the basic "takeaway" message for you?

THE
SuperGaL
syndrome
Breaking the Chains of Control, Pride & Perfectionism™

Busy, burdened women—moms, wives, neighbors, coworkers—are increasingly suffering from the debilitating side effects of superhero complex, known as *The SuperGal Syndrome*. This spiritual disease has become epidemic among women of all ages, negatively impacting our families, friends and fellow believers.

Fueled by her passion to inspire women who struggle in their self-imposed chains, Lori Hynson shares her SuperGal Recovery secrets through the Word of God. With joy, transparency, humor, and song, Lori reaches out to hurting and overburdened women to encourage them to surrender these burdensome chains to God. She wants them to realize, as she has had to learn, that IT'S NOT OUR JOB TO RUN THIS PLANET!!

To book Lori for your next event, go to www.lorihynson.com or write to her at supergal@lorihynson.com

For more on *SuperGal vs. GOD*, visit www.lorihynson.com

www.ingramcontent.com/pod-product-compliance
Lightning Source LLC
LaVergne TN
LVHW051817080426
835513LV00017B/1990